NLP

Utilizing Efficient Methods Such As Speed Reading, Subliminal Persuasion, And Mind Control To Influence Individuals Effectively

(The Success Of NLP As A Scientific Discipline For Human Interaction)

Nicola Christiansen

TABLE OF CONTNET

Gradient-Based Expression 1

Aiming To Push People To Higher Levels Of Interpersonal Communication Via Meta Model And Meta Model Violations 10

The Quick Phobia Cure Nlp Method 29

Interpreting Spoken Words 40

Which Values Do You Uphold? 59

Dark Persuasion Strategies To Watch Out For 88

Securing 117

Gradient-Based Expression

A person vibrates beautifully with the universe when they are feeling grateful. Put another way, one is vibrating at such a high frequency that everything, including conditions and events, depends on what one is searching for or how it seems. Generally speaking, you may not attract what you desire if you are accustomed to fighting yourself. It is crucial to realize that one's emotions and perception of life shape one's mindset and define life.

Most of the time, one's opinions are a product of stored memories. As a result, you must feed your mind with relevant life experiences so that none of your judgments are harmful to other people.

Concentrate on improving your memory with smart minds. This factor has to do with the idea that positive perceptions are always formed when one feeds their spirit with pleasant thoughts. The feature also conjures up an image that sees reality differently in the mind. Setting your sights on greatness is crucial. Put another way, if you feed your spirits with renown, there's a good chance you'll meet great people and eventually become great yourself. Rewriting the negative aspects of your attitude is what you will do when you concentrate on being grateful. Put another way, one paints images of life that are positive.

This component of life typically manifests itself in one's overall actions. You will quickly establish a connection with brilliant brains if you maintain your focus and think positively. In life, mental images are vital. The feature represents both the things we have been exposed to and the things we have taken in. To think positively, it is essential to conjure up positive mental images. All the specifics and the index's behaviors are gratefully geared toward excellence. As a result, develop an appreciation for your mind and assist in forming more optimistic mental images. The element is vital since it lets one concentrate and let go of life's bad aspects.

Choose

You must take action to get complete clarity on your goals, what you want to achieve, and what, in your opinion, would be the key to an outstanding existence. Your vision will get stronger the more consideration you give it, and the more detail you lay out, the more powerful it will be. It also generates an unconscious mind map that gives your brain the resources to realize that vision. Decide that you will not settle and are unprepared to live as you currently do. Then, focus on what you want and start rewiring your mind. The next step in reprogramming is to commit to your decision, let it guide you, and free yourself from self-doubt and fear. One of the main obstacles that will prevent you from acting is fear. If you don't take action, that fear will stay exactly where it is, obstructing your way, and you won't move. While you won't perform any better, you also won't perform any worse. And that fear will constantly lurk in the background of your thoughts, preventing you from achieving your objectives. If you do nothing, the negativity will have more time to contaminate your thoughts and eventually infiltrate your unconscious mind, influencing your actions and self-perception. You must commit to improving your life and to yourself by conquering negativity. The true power of unconscious mind programming is that it allows you to demand more of yourself than anybody else could imagine when you engage and close off all other possibilities.

Giving the reprogramming process enough time to complete its task is crucial. It is important to remember that you shouldn't count on seeing improvements in your life right away. Sometimes, perhaps, it can help cultivate some of these wonderful parts of life; most of the time, though, it takes time. As a result, you might need to teach some optimism in yourself. The feature allows your brain to absorb life's good aspects and let go of its bad ones. It is important to remember that thinking acts or functions in the same way as feeding. Put another way; it records many negative concerns and forms such a view if subjected to negativity. Therefore, instead of forcing your unconscious mind to comply with your wishes, consider applying the strategies with a kind and curious attitude. Once you have decided and committed to the road, assess the current state of affairs. Not every challenge, hardship, or situation is the same; each has its own set of challenges that you can overcome. The true power is within, and you can rewire your unconscious thinking to become successful. You are about to make a breakthrough while you are frustrated. Failure is a teaching tool, offering advice on improving and moving forward. Every obstacle presents a chance for you to change course and develop an original, creative answer. The use of your thoughts is the other essential component. Refrain from being inactive. Idleness breeds pessimistic ideas, which erode the ability to retain happy memories. Therefore, learn to invest in optimistic thinking even if facing life challenges.

You should start learning about pacing and leading right now. Think about it like this. Pacing is adopting the mental attitude of another person. Some people are so joyful that it spreads to everyone around them, making them happy as a byproduct of their positive attitude. It all comes down to attitude. It can either brighten our day and make us feel good or depress and frustrate us. Pacing is joining in on someone else's emotional state and returning the favor. Similar to how mirroring and mimicking people's physical behaviors helps establish rapport, this offers more: it allows us to set the example for behavior.

After you have placed someone, you want to gently influence that person's behavior and mental state to take a different turn. This is when you are leading. You could pace their neutrality by beginning neutral. Joining them in a frame of mind where they are not overtly happy or negative is what I mean. At that point, you might begin to grin, laugh a little, and eventually develop a genuinely positive attitude and state of mind. Now, you have helped illuminate the room, so to speak, and transformed them from apathetic to exuberant happiness. And that makes me happy!

The lesson has concluded. Today's task is to merely incorporate this knowledge into your conversations with other people on an interpersonal level. Practice, practice, and more practice.

Aiming To Push People To Higher Levels Of Interpersonal Communication Via Meta Model And Meta Model Violations

As explained in a previous lecture, the initial founders of NLP were Drs. John Grinder and Richard Bandler. They examined successful people by examining their speech patterns and, more precisely, their words from a linguistic standpoint. The works of luminaries like Virginia Satire and Dr. Milton Erickson were examined. Grinder and Bandler developed communication models to illustrate the structure of their language and methodology.

Milton Erickson, in particular, was portrayed as having a lot of ambiguities, deletions, generalizations, and other creatively ambiguous language patterns, mostly related to his use of indirect hypnosis in psychotherapy sessions with his patients.

One could conceptualize the Meta Model as the Milton Model's opposite. That's not quite accurate, but the Meta Model aims to explain these language phenomena that arise in everyday speech. It's rather clever since it can quickly shift perspectives, which can cause assumptions to change. As was previously explained, beliefs are the judgments we make about how things ought to be. They help us make sense of things from "a" perspective that has evolved and defines and constrains us. In addition to providing people with a sense of safety, status, meaning, reality, and so forth, beliefs can also restrict our thinking, create falsity, persuade us to believe lies and have the opposite effect.

For a split second, picture someone approaching you and declaring, "He hates me." I will never be worthy enough to please him. I fail every time I attempt.

Given that I haven't provided you with enough background or knowledge to fully comprehend the circumstances surrounding the creation of this monologue, it is understandable that some questions may arise and answers may be needed. You might have conjured up some images, brought up feelings or ideas from the past, or recalled something vaguely related to this monologue. If so, that's OK; if not, that's also acceptable. I want you to realize that the speech above is ambiguous, leaves out important details, and involves judgment. This outburst is typical (or typical behavior) in everyday interactions. The Meta Model helps NLPers (like ourselves) to "get to the bottom of things" by interpreting these kinds of subtleties in communication and, in effect, "calling a person out" or "challenging their statements" or posing questions to verify clarity. Clarity eliminates any room for ambiguity to obscure our meaning. One of the NLP tenets is that "the meaning of communication is the affect it has by the receiver, not the message intended by the messenger." You may remember this from a prior course. You may be sensing by now that messages are constantly misinterpreted by different messengers. Listen to the news and observe how different news programs present the same "objective" information, but the message is not the same because of how it was presented to the viewers.

Returning to my earlier example: When somebody expresses, "He hates me." "Who is he?" is the first question that needs to be clarified. Is this because "he" is an ambiguous noun that leaves the message recipient in the dark as to who "he" is? What precisely is it that 'he' dislikes about you? This is the second inquiry an NLPer should consider asking. We pose this question because the verb "hate" is not specified because it lacks a reference point. I'll end this example here for now, but I wanted to give you this overview so you could understand the general direction of the NLP Meta Model. It's important to realize that the speaker of this statement is not conveying their meaning concisely and enough for the listener to understand what is intended.

I want to clarify that there are situations in which imprecise, unclear, indistinct, and indirect language can be helpful before I teach you the NLP META MODEL. It is appropriate in various settings, including counseling, sales, motivational speaking, speeches, ministering, etc. Therefore, please don't get caught up in the idea that you have to dissect every conversation someone has with you to extract the information that needs to be extracted as clearly as possible. It's not always required. In my view, NLP helps provide you with this perspective on communication, which you can then use to help people, be more direct, and be able to solve complex communication problems with individuals or in groups when needed or beneficial – for example, when you need to classify information and make sense of the absurd.

During my initial days of studying NLP, I had a challenging notion. I wondered, "What does metal mean?" I tried my best to understand instinctively and even looked up the solution on Google and in several NLP books. Eventually, I discovered that the word "meta" is a Greek word that implies "about" or "above"; it functions as a catch-all for anything that lies beneath the surface of our comprehension. The implementation of this NLP metamodel aligns with the majority of sales scenarios. In my opinion, this is the main justification for every sales professional to dedicate themselves to mastering the metamodel. You may wonder what this main application is. As there are numerous ways to overlook what is happening in another person's inner structure, the application is just to help us understand what someone else is trying to say. When individuals communicate, they often use words that erase, distort, and generalize meanings. Despite appearing entirely reasonable and intelligible, their comments may include much grammatical ambiguity. Based on their understanding of the world, the listener or message recipient deduces what is intended. As a result, there are problems with communication.

Sales professionals can comprehensively comprehend the meaning of a communication, namely its deep structure, by mastering the metamodel. When this occurs, the salesperson is more in line with the possible client's requirements, preferences, and wishes. With an understanding of this metamodel, a sales professional can ask needs development and awareness questions to find not just the logical needs but also the emotional needs of a potential customer.

Which Benefits Can You Gain from Manipulation?

Manipulation has a negative connotation. We often hear about manipulation in a negative light, knowing that the manipulator gets to go off and enjoy what they want while the target is harmed or causes problems for others. In certain situations, this is the only thing manipulation is about.

On the other hand, there are situations in which manipulation is beneficial. Making sure the target receives the vehicle they desire is the purpose of a salesperson trying to close a deal. Manipulation may be used by a family member attempting to get their drug-addicted child into therapy to obtain the necessary care and support. Furthermore, some sort of manipulation will always be involved if you have ever heard a pitch for a fundraiser or charitable cause.

Manipulation has the potential to yield several worthwhile advantages. Whether you are using manipulation for good or evil, you will discover that both the manipulator and, occasionally, the target can experience many benefits from the process. The following are a few advantages of utilizing manipulation:

Can assist you in achieving your goals

The idea and technique of manipulation appeal to people primarily because it allows them to achieve their desired outcomes. Knowing that you can enter any room, speak with whomever you like, and persuade them to agree or behave as you choose can make a tremendous difference in a world where wants exist beyond time. Many people are curious to learn more about it since it seems so appealing, but not everyone has the skills to make it all come true. Whatever you hope to gain via manipulating someone else won't matter since it will bring you there. Manipulation can be useful whether or not your intentions are good. It could be something small, like getting assistance with a project or getting lunch when you're too busy to leave the office, or it could be something a lot more. You will be able to achieve your goals with the aid of manipulation.

Can Increase Your Self-Assurance

Working with manipulation can be a really helpful tool for you to help yourself become more confident. Frequently, we forfeit our desires due to our shyness or excessive concern about other people's opinions of us. Even if we don't know what to do when the other person tells us no regarding something, we can be afraid that they will say no to us.

On the other hand, you will acquire the necessary skills while working with manipulation to ensure you receive what you desire. You'll discover the words and actions you must use to guarantee your target will always agree. If you know that you can go into any room and, no matter what you ask, find someone to agree with you, just picture how much more confidence-boosting it would be.

Can assist you in obtaining the relationship you desire

You may occasionally employ manipulation to secure the kind of connection you desire and persuade someone to go on a date with you. This may relieve individuals who have previously struggled to locate someone with whom to go out. Perhaps all you need to convince someone to go out with you is some self-assurance and communication skills.

This doesn't have to be something cunning or malevolent. Furthermore, that won't be the greatest method to start a new relationship. But you can utilize some of the strategies we'll cover in this handbook to assist you in starting that relationship.

For instance, you can employ several strategies if there's someone you're interested in. Perhaps you begin spending more time with them in a thought-provoking environment to become more at ease with one another and discover more about their preferences. This might assist you in customizing your message to best fit that person's characteristics.

The foot-in-the-door method is an additional option to consider. Here's where you start by acclimating them to several modest requests so they develop the habit of accepting you. You may gently ask them out by asking for assistance with a project, getting their opinion on your dependability, and finally, asking if they would be open to going out with you. You are more likely to obtain the date you desire when you make that bold request, especially after you have spent some time convincing that person to say yes to you.

Can Help the Other Individual

You will discover that using manipulation appropriately may be advantageous to both the target and you. There are two primary kinds of manipulation; some just serve the interests of the manipulator, while others have the potential to be advantageous to all parties.

The manipulator will only attempt to obtain advantages for the first group.

What happens to the target is irrelevant to them. If the manipulator can obtain what they want from the circumstance, they might be OK with harming or taking advantage of the target. The target may find this difficult. They frequently endure years of cruelty and mistreatment before realizing the manipulator is in their lives.

In these circumstances, the manipulator has created an environment where the target feels forced to follow them. This is a case of codependency when the target is more than happy to comply with the manipulator's wishes, even if they don't always benefit from them. This kind of scenario can be difficult to resolve and may take several years to improve.

The manipulator is a little more discreet in the second scenario. Even though this is a necessary component of the venture, they won't concentrate as much on obtaining what they want. Although the manipulator will get what they want, the target will succeed in this scenario. In this case, the manipulator will aim to do something that will assist and benefit the target rather than destroy the objective.

An outstanding illustration of this is a salesperson. The target will have to deal with manipulation if they go out for an automobile. Perhaps the priceiest one they can find, as this will increase their compensation. They will force their will on the target, who will then have the option of accepting or rejecting the car.

The Quick Phobia Cure Nlp Method

This method is commonly referred to as dissociation in NLP. One highly useful NLP approach for getting rid of painful memories that give rise to phobias is dissociation. For example, a high fall that you or someone else experienced in the past may be the cause of your acrophobia or fear of heights. The severe aversion to animals known as zoophobia may have resulted from an encounter in which you witnessed or experienced an animal attack or murder.

The source of your fear, dissociation therapy can help you overcome phobias. Dissociation facilitates the separation of your mental images from the emotions they evoke. It makes you feel safer, calmer, and more capable of viewing things from a new angle and changing your mind about certain issues.

Your brain is rewired through dissociation, which limits the trigger of your fight-or-flight response when it comes to the subject of your phobia.

The Method of Embedded Commands

Embedded directives are another tactic used by salespeople and marketers to elicit customers' desired responses.

This method functions similarly to the mirroring method's supporting role. Once you've mirrored someone and gained their trust, you can employ embedded commands to elicit a positive response.

Embedded commands are commands that are covered up and hidden within words. For example, there is an implicit command in a remark such as "You can feel good as you start this next exercise."

The Method of Modelling

Modeling is emulating positive attitudes and behaviors. For example, if you'd like to take over as CEO of your company and you think highly of the current CEO, you could start acting like them.

Through modeling, you can learn skills to help you perform better, understand others better, and improve subpar performances.

The Technique of Empowering Questions

The questions that empower the foundation of the NLP technique are based on the idea that it can enhance your quality of life.

Asking a question that empowers you, like "What have I learned from what has happened to me?" will yield greater results than asking, "Why is this happening to me?"

The former leaves you feeling bad, unhappy, and hopeless; the latter teaches you how to keep from repeating the same mistakes and improves your performance in the future. Asking empowering questions can help you look forward to a better future instead of dwelling on the past.

The Fast-Paced Future Method

One mental imagery technique that can help you relate changes to future circumstances is called future pacing. You can use the future pacing technique, for example, to improve your performance at a given task in the future.

To guarantee the new result you wish to experience is established, future pacing typically occurs after an NLP technique process. Visualizing future circumstances makes it simpler to achieve the desired outcome when those circumstances arise.

For example, you can fast-forward to a future time when you see dogs and, instead of being afraid, you play with them, feed them, and feel comfortable around them.

The Sets of Yes

consistency and congruence between their actions and words. Under the pretense of daring or claiming to be capable of doing something, they will act in ways they ordinarily wouldn't. People try their hardest not to be inconsistent in public because they detest appearing inconsistent and are afraid of what other people will think. This is essentially where the yes set's power resides. That and the tendency for those who say yes to continue saying so, in the same way that motion tends to stay motion; this represents an additional mental shortcut that our brain employs. Overall, though, you will greatly benefit from it.

One of the most basic patterns you can use is the Yes Set. After you've asked someone three questions, you know they'll say "yes," so you ask them the one you want them to answer. A lot of people think this is just an outdated sales ploy. The psychological underpinnings of the yes-set, however, have been a functional component of hypnosis, psychology, therapy, and many other forms of communication. A person can and will do what you want them to do if you pace them into an agreement with you and know where to take the conversation.

Are you starting to grasp what the yes-set is?

Do you think you would use it?

Is it not the case that this tactic can effectively lead someone along the gradual path of persuasion?

When you put the strategies you're learning into practice, will you be prepared to do so?

That is all. That's all it takes, and it's a really powerful way to get someone to say yes to you.

However, as with anything, you won't achieve the same results if you try to force the yes set into a conversational topic it doesn't belong in, come across as manipulative, or are overly direct. There is a place and a time for using hypnotic language in conversation, just like with everything else we've discussed.

They make excellent transitional tools for the yes crowd. In other words, they work well when you redirect someone's attention and move them from a certain place. They also allow you to seize control of the Frame immediately and use it for both your and their advantage, much like many techniques.

It can establish rapport, bring up small talk, start a conversation, and move it from where the other person is mentally to the point of business. This is an excellent method of encouraging others to get to work and get ready to write things down for you.

After that, it functions as an excellent conventional form that moves from one topic of discussion to another. In sales, you can ensure the customer knows the product before discussing pricing or going from pricing to purchase. You can use it as a tool in other influence efforts to summarise what you believe they should be doing and what you believe they understand about you. This can always turn into a special method to advance the conversation gracefully while also giving the other person the impression that you're taking your time to ensure you understand each other.

Interpreting Spoken Words

In this chapter, We will examine how verbal communication functions in interpersonal communication. These concepts will assist you in concentrating on how your tone of voice and the words you choose might express a particular thought.

Speaking is probably the most common way of verbal communication. This indicates that humans make noises with their voices. The brain then assigns meaning to these sounds after decoding them. A sound is essentially meaningless if it has no associated meaning.

The basis of language is this. A unique system learned through time decodes the meaning tied to each sound and sign that makes up language. Every language is made up of a variety of systems for denoting these sounds. Thus, the English language is a system in which the brain interprets sounds and decodes them to determine meaning.

It takes children many years of instruction and training to master the foundations of language since language is so complicated. After that, a person needs even more time to acquire complete language proficiency. There are PhDs and master's degrees specifically focused on specific languages. That is how extensive a scope of knowledge a single language can be.

It should be acknowledged that language has two dimensions: written and spoken. This chapter will focus on the oral component of language, as written communication is not part of the purview that applies to this book. Although it is an interesting field, comprehending written communication calls for an entirely other strategy, which takes us away from the primary focus of this book.

Oral communication is, therefore, the main way that people communicate. Newborns even use oral communication to express their feelings. An infant, for instance, will cry to let their caregiver know they're in trouble. Of course, that discomfort can be anything from a soggy diaper to hunger. Still, a newborn can communicate verbally and understand what is being said.

Language acquisition takes precedence over other subjects as one's cognitive abilities advance. Speaking correctly is emphasized heavily in basic schooling, even if other subjects like math and reading comprehension are also important. Communicating effectively through speech gives children and adults the means to express themselves more fully and share their thoughts with those around them.

For this reason, language serves as the primary means of oral communication. Meaning is assigned to sounds and utterances. These interpretations are promptly tested after being learned. Communication occurs when others understand these noises. Communication breaks down if these noises are not successfully decoded for whatever reason.

Oral communication is based on this idea about sounds and how to decode them.

In what way?

Consider the proverb, "It's not what you say; it's how you say it."

The tone, pitch, and even timbre of your voice will all intrinsically impact the meaning you transmit when communicating orally. You can see how important it might be to gain a proper hold over your voice if you pay attention to these factors.

One well-known instance is speaking up. What message are you sending to your opponent when you raise your voice?

Raising your voice during a quarrel may indicate the conversation is getting more intense. It could also be interpreted as an aggressive gesture in which your opponent might decide to go on the defensive. If not handled properly, this could spark a dispute.

On the other hand, speaking louder may be seen as an indication of approaching danger. For example, if you yell, "watch out," people nearby won't likely perceive it as aggressive behavior. On the contrary, they will go on the defensive in reaction to the threat you have pointed out.

Years and years of work are required to master these minute details. These are not innate abilities that children possess from birth. They are taught in schools for this reason. Children need to be schooled in several areas to properly integrate into their social environment.

To help their pupils convey the appropriate message, professional trainers and coaches have created courses and programs that teach them how to master their voice. Radio hosts and television newscasters must complete some training to be proficient communicators. If not, they might unintentionally make mistakes when transmitting.

Accent neutralization is the most typical instruction that newscasters receive. Although there is nothing wrong with a person's original accent, not all possible listeners may be familiar with its inflections. Therefore, accent training is required to have a flat, neutral tone that everyone listening may understand more easily.

Keeping that in mind, let's examine the different facets of oral communication. By being acutely aware of these factors, you may adjust your voice to best fit your communication goals. Specifically, you can adjust the pitch of your voice to fit the context and the scenario.

Ultimately, delivering a speech at a funeral is one thing, but it is quite another to make a sales pitch.

We will start by examining tone as our first element.

As mentioned, speaking up can be interpreted as a threat or aggressiveness. Conversely, speaking in a lower volume can indicate that you are discussing private information or do not want others to hear you.

Additionally, a lower voice tone may convey a calm and tranquil tone when attempting to defuse a crisis. For example, you can respond with a flat, even tone if the other person is becoming more aggressive. All you are doing is stopping the confrontation from worsening, even if you are hardly giving in.

When you are giving a speech or making a presentation, it is quite beneficial to use an even tone. While most trainers will tell you that you must display emotion (which is true to some extent), keeping your tone neutral will convey to your audience that you are in charge and knowledgeable about the subject at hand.

It is important to note that you can experiment with the pitch in your voice when it comes to expressing emotion, particularly while making a sales pitch.

A higher or lower register in your voice is referred to as pitch. Whether you sound like Darth Vader or have a squeaky voice, you can still experiment with the pitch of your voice. You may indeed convey your emotions through the pitch.

For example, if you were giving a serious speech or speaking at a funeral, you might think about speaking at a lower pitch. On the other hand, if you are delivering good news or making a sales presentation, you can utilize a higher pitch.

Pitch is, therefore, crucial in expressing emotion. Naturally, you want to exercise caution to avoid going overboard. When people are thrilled, most go a little too far and speak in a high, squeaky voice. Additionally, some people talk monotonely, even in a happy and joyous atmosphere. These folks are viewed as dull and monotonous in such situations. It is crucial to understand your surroundings and any implications that may arise.

In addition to pitch, intonation is crucial for effectively conveying information. There are two primary types of intonation: rising and decreasing. As a result, you can employ rising or lowering intonation based on the circumstance.

Generally speaking, rising intonation is employed while posing a question to get a response. These days, questions differ in syntax depending on the language. However, most languages indicate that you need a response by employing rising intonation at the end of a sentence.

Do you want something to drink? for instance, it might sound more like, "Do you want something to DRINK?" The word "drink" has a rising tone, as shown by the caps, suggesting that your counterpart must respond.

You can end a conversation by using a falling intonation. This lets your conversation partner know they are welcome to join in. You risk leaving your opponent hanging if you don't give them a suitable indication that you're done speaking. They can get perplexed since they won't know if you're done talking or still have something to say.

For example, a sentence like "Let's go to the movies" should end with a dropping intonation since you are finished speaking. Your opponent would then react appropriately. Similarly, your opponent will indicate whether they agree or disagree with you by using a dropping intonation in their response.

But your conversation partner might answer this with a query like "now?" In this situation, your counterpart must know if you plan to leave immediately or later. What this accomplishes is giving you the choice of responding or not. All of these interactions, of course, appear to be quite typical. However, they could confuse others who speak languages with different patterns. Therefore, it is essential to comprehend these non-linguistic cues to communicate effectively.

What Are Your Thoughts?

You're prepared to examine yourself. You might wish to get a notepad if you enjoy making lists and writing things down. It can be useful to jot down the answers to your many questions.

First, you will be asked to consider your self-perception. This will assist you in comprehending your concept of yourself. We'll enquire about your worldviews as well. When discussing relationships and communication later in the chapter, these questions will help us improve at NLP. Now is the time to put on your thinking cap!

Respond to the following inquiries:

*Is your physique in decent shape? If so, what is the reason?

Determine which aspects of your appearance you find most appealing. Consider the good things about the way you look.

If not, what would be the reason?

Make an effort to tell the truth, but don't compromise. If your weight is unhealthy, be upfront about it!

Do you wish to enhance your outward look? How can you accomplish that?*Are you drawn to your personality?

If so, what is the reason?

- Are you morally upright? What attributes make someone a decent person, in your opinion? Do you think that other people like you? What quality about you appeals to other people?

If not, what would be the reason?

- Do you have personal flaws? What weaknesses do you think you have? Treat your body with kindness and honesty. Are you a grumpy or easily irritated person? What would you say if you asked someone to characterize a weakness in your personality?*Do you speak positively or negatively to yourself?

-Who is the voice inside you?

What is the tone in which you conduct your inner monologues? Do you think well of yourself or poorly of yourself? Do you tend to be pessimistic, minimizing your accomplishments, or can you adequately congratulate yourself when you succeed?

How does your inner voice appear and sound?

- Can you talk to yourself in your voice and tone, or do you let other people's mannerisms and inflections—like those of a parent, teacher, or other powerful person—dictate your inner monologue?*Beyond your convictions, what can you believe?

-Are you spiritual or religious in your beliefs?

Do you think a deity, gods, or other greater power exists?

- Why? Do you think that God exists? Or did you happen to stumble across your faith? Why not? Do you place your trust and confidence in material objects?

- Do you adhere to political principles firmly?

- Which side do you support—liberalism, conservatism, or both? What circumstances led you to form those beliefs? Did you establish these views, or did your parents pass them down?

- Do you dislike those who hold different opinions or believe they are always incorrect? Are you willing to discuss or learn about different points of view?* Do you believe that humans are nice or bad in general?

Why, in your opinion, are humans good? Do you view people's best qualities as an optimist?

- Why do you believe that humans are bad? Do you draw your conclusions from firsthand experience or general observation?* Do you think that change can be brought about amicably and without violence?

- Can you communicate effectively?

If so, what characteristics help you communicate effectively?

-Do you think you possess the necessary communication skills?

Which Values Do You Uphold?

What attributes would you like to incorporate into your daily existence?

- Are you someone who values family? Respect, loyalty, and integrity? Do you consider money and material belongings to be important? Are you motivated by rivalry and ambition?

-How do you incorporate your principles into your day-to-day activities? Do you find it difficult to live up to your values?

- Are your values a source of satisfaction or concern for you?

Are you trying to find someone who shares your values?

- Do your friends and family share the same values? Or does your group of pals consist of a variety of people?

Do your studies and work match your values and beliefs? Do you have trouble locating the ideal job?*Considering your responses thus far, would you say you're generally happy with your life?

- Why? Think about all the little things in your life that make you happy.

Which facets of your life make you happy? Do you think there are answers? These are supposed to be challenging questions that will challenge your thinking. Together, your responses will paint a portrait of who you are. It will highlight your desired qualities and personality traits in others. It will also make your worldview clear. This is how you see yourself. Your views, values, and sense of self-worth are contained within. The elegance of neuro-linguistic programming lies in this. You can utilize it to reach where you want to go, create objectives for your ambitions, and be anyone you want. Let's examine one last instance of NLP enhancing self-perception. This one is about transforming your perception by others. You can use this activity to help you get ready for the upcoming subjects. In the upcoming chapters, we'll talk about using NLP to connect, influence, and communicate with people.

You will be asked to consider your responses to how other people see you in this activity. How did you feel? There are various ways to approach this subject. It may seem a little morbid, but it works. If you passed away tomorrow, what would you say to your loved ones? Almost everyone has occasionally thought something like this. Why do you suppose they won't compliment you? Do you think you're not worthy, or are you denying yourself the chance?

If you don't think well of yourself and have a poor self-concept, you can think that people dislike you. Seeing how other people perceive you when you're feeling down about yourself can be challenging. It may also be difficult for you to realize that others might value you more than you do if you suffer from conditions like anxiety or depression.

Questions concerning your personality and the opinions of others were posed to you. This compelled you to think about every component of who you are. It would not be hard to find something in your answers to the previous questions that you disagree with. Since everyone is fallible, there's always room for improvement. NLP can assist, regardless of the reason(s), you may believe that people dislike. Self-image and modifying any unfavorable traits that might be preventing you.

Let's begin with a visualization exercise designed to boost your self-esteem. This calls for a shift in language and images. Relax and close your eyes. First, you'll look in a full-length mirror at yourself. Think about your self-perception that goes beyond your appearance and little imperfections. You will learn more about your genuine self-worth and self-esteem with this practice.

Then, put your thoughts about yourself into words. Visualize them suspended in midair. Imagine yourself grabbing the encouraging remarks and letting go of the negative ones as they do. You can picture yourself eliminating all bad thoughts and holding onto just good ones. Imagine the scene often to remind yourself not to allow depressing emotions to creep in.

Since NLP is personal, you can picture eliminating your self-defeating ideas in any way that works for you. Envision yourself within a batting cage, and visualize your pessimistic ideas being vanquished. You can kick the things that upset you while wearing boots. Whatever it takes to rid yourself of your bad emotions doesn't matter. Make it memorable.

When I say, "We are going swimming, and then we will have lunch," our minds only focus on the part of the sentence before the word "and." In contrast, this is not the case when I say, "We are going swimming." However, all the mind would hear is that we are going to eat lunch if I reworded the sentence to say, "We are going to have lunch, and before that we will go swimming."

But in NLP, words aren't the only thing that has power. Touch is equally significant. A few strategically placed pats on the upper arm during a talk will help a new communication partner feel comfortable enough to trust you sooner rather than later while you're developing rapport (creating trust).

Pacing is the last NLP tactic to be aware of. Pacing means that you provide your communication partner, say, three concrete facts, and then you present the idea that you want them to accept as true. The sentence "Our boss is on leave today (first fact), and she took the secretaries with her (second fact)" is an example of a pacing script. However, the CEO is present (third factual statement). Our boss is constantly on leave (incorrect fact)." Your communicative partner is more likely to take the untrue fact as gospel truth since you introduced the untrue fact—that your boss is always on leave—with two or three clear facts.

Applications of NLP

Dark manipulation is not the primary application for natural language processing (NLP). In actuality, NLP is applied to personal development and enhancement. You can rewire your mind using the earlier approaches to become a better version of yourself. Visualization lets you quickly alter your pessimistic views of life and begin to see things positively. It is crucial to remember that NLP is a self-improvement tool that can boost your cognitive function and help you regain your sense of self.

NLP is used to foster a variety of abilities, including confidence, communication, and self-reflection. NLP can help you succeed in your professional endeavors and your interpersonal interactions. If you apply the strategies correctly, you will gain clout as a leader and ascend easily to a position of authority in your workplace.

It is necessary to discuss the negative aspects of NLP. There's a significant risk involved with the language since it can cause a complete reprogramming of the mind. NLP can be a harmful tool since it can be used to influence people and learn about their ideas. You should intend to advance if you wish to practice NLP. Growth and increased productivity ought to be your top priorities. You must set aside your egotistical goals and concentrate on what's best for the majority. NLP can be used to assist those you work with or subordinates in reaching their greatest potential. NLP can also help you perform better personally and interact more socially with others in your company.

NLP is widely used in medicine, particularly in the treatment of mental illnesses. It can be applied to assist those who are depressed and anxious. For the majority of those people, anxiety, terror, and panic attacks are only brought on by certain circumstances that remind them of the past. You can assist those people in altering their emotional associations by using the NLP approach. You can assist kids in beginning to associate specific situations with favorable responses rather than unfavorable ones. Patients with anxiety and despair may find that the sensory association with specific triggers improves their overall perspective on life.

Patients with PTSD have also been reported to benefit from NLP. Anybody who has had horrific occurrences in their lives could have an extremely unrealistic outlook on life. For those people, negativity becomes an enduring aspect of their existence. If you learn how to apply NLP, you can develop bonds with those people, gather the necessary data, and utilize it to rewire the targets' thoughts.

Chapter 5: Techniques of Manipulation

P

Psychological coercion is a type of social control that uses deceptive, deceptive, or indirect methods to try and change other people's behavior or opinions. These tactics could be deceptive and exploitative since they advance the manipulator's goals, sometimes to the disadvantage of others.

External influences don't necessarily have negative consequences. Individuals such as coworkers, family members, and medical professionals may try to persuade others to change blatantly counterproductive beliefs and actions. Since external power respects the influence's freedom to accept or reject it and is not overly oppressive, it is typically seen as benign. Social control may be considered dishonest bribery under certain circumstances and with certain intentions.

Indications That Someone Is Trying to Harm You With Psychological Coercion

It can be challenging to distinguish between psychological abuse and other forms of abuse, regardless of how long you have been engaging in this kind of exploitation, mostly because the real masters of mental camouflage are the manipulators themselves.

Usually, their polite conversation conceals their destructive, cynical, and self-serving ideas. Apart from this conflicting collision of words and deeds, they also aim to provoke strong feelings of regret or sympathy in their opponents to make them more susceptible to manipulation.

Psychological manipulators cause you to question all of your feelings and emotions. It's common to refer to this engineering technique as "gaslighting." As Stephanie A. Sarkis, Ph. D., the author of Psychology Today, puts it, gaslighting is "a technique through which an individual or group is manipulating their truth through the attempt to obtain more control." Because they are always cunning and well-informed, their deceptive tactics can occasionally go undiscovered. Conscious and dynamic patterns of reasoning are necessary for manipulation, and they can only be achieved by someone who takes advantage of human nature.

"Psychological coercion is when one person is used for the benefit of another. The manipulator purposely creates a power gap and uses the target to further his or her purpose," explains Professor Preston Ni in more detail. "How do you know if someone is mentally exploiting you?" asks Professor Ni. It can be difficult to identify their sophisticated tactics. Thus, your best ally will always be your instincts or "positive feelings."

But if you're not the type to believe in your gut, these four signs are serious red flags of psychological abuse in a relationship:

1. You will be duped by their "expert expertise."

These people attempt to trick you with so-called "evidence" or "statistical details." Manipulators are doing this to demonstrate their analytical superiority, even if it's all made-up bullshit. Are the authorities in that domain? Naturally, it isn't. But they would have you believe otherwise. They usually have a somewhat disproportionate experience with a wide range of people or events, and they never miss an opportunity to flaunt their skills when the time is right. Anything that comes to mind can instantly change how deeply they feel about a particular subject.

Have you been having fantasies about getting a new car? Don't be duped if you know the ideal build and layout for your particular requirements. Do you have any plans to take a ride somewhere? They will advise you of all the top places to stay for top-notch dining. And yes, they only focus on this fantastic and helpful content because they need to.

Many dishonest individuals in our environment are essentially practitioners of none and mere jacks of all trades. However, certain "experts in their field" are extraordinarily intelligent and possess a manipulative intelligence that makes them especially hazardous to deal with.

It's obvious that in this situation, you should use caution. If someone controls every conversation you're trying to have, immediately shift the focus to them. I understand that you're probably not the kind to confront people or cause trouble, but there are instances when you just have to say no.

You should leave the situation in silence if you lack the will or courage to confront the manipulator for being too deceitful. Give them a little time to talk to each other.

2. You're under pressure from them to make decisions.

Which occurs when you decide quickly? If we give it a few minutes of consideration, it sometimes doesn't work as well as it should. Weighing our choices and employing the knowledge we have gathered to make a choice is one of our largest benefits toward (as they know) a psychological manipulator. They are attempting to persuade you to respond to their worries or act decisively when under duress. "I have to do this by..." "This is due, and I need..." "If this doesn't happen soon, I'm trying to..." and so on are examples of how they are attempting to convey a sense of urgency.

By the way, I've encountered people with this mentality rather frequently, particularly obnoxious salespeople and business travelers. We will only keep putting pressure on you to buy their products, acting like the universe will end tomorrow, even though you didn't. It's awful! My politeness has kept me from seizing the darn thing and giving it a hefty slap on the ear!

The best thing you can do when you start to feel under pressure to make a decision or notice that your anxiety is suddenly increasing is to say, "Not now." Suppose you can say it 100 times. Just be firm and tell them that you won't be coerced or threatened into doing anything you're not sure you want to do.

3. Guilt trips are what they're using to get you to do something for them.

If you are a sensitive or empathic person, this is the most stressful psychological manipulation you will experience. Manipulators can use guilt trips and passive-aggressive comments as useful tools. Guy Winch, Ph., a writer for Psychology Today, describes a guilt trip as a manipulative strategy when the manipulator tries to incite the victim's excessive sense of regret to exert control over them. They will use any combination of these strategies to get you to do nearly anything.

4. They're turning to furious outbursts.

You might want to brace for an adult tantrum if something doesn't go their way or you bring up their bad behavior. At times, these outbursts of rage grow silent and unnoticed as the person witnessing them acts as though they are unaware of the uncomfortable circumstances they are facing. However, there are times when they could be even more harmful and unpleasant.

Psychological manipulators will stop at nothing to get what they want and will resort to aggressive behavior, nasty language, or even violent outbursts if at all feasible. They know that if they go crazy, they will get what they want, so they start slamming doors, tossing things, and calling names.

It is not a good aspect of any friendship, so get help if you're afraid of being physically abused. Talk to a trusted family member or relative who will support your decision to move away and simplify your life. Whatever you do, don't let the negative mindset you've encountered go unspoken.

It's time for you to take action if you believe that you are connected to a sexual manipulator.

All we do is decide what matters to us and the people we care about. However, remember that this is one of the most important things you will do to take charge of your mental and emotional health. Don't allow someone to undermine or take away who you truly are. Look for someone who will support you, or even better, place a wager with them!

In the corporate world, dealing with dishonest coworkers is not whether you will encounter them but where and how you will handle the situation.

There are dishonest peers in every industry, profession, level of skill, and business, and if they are driven enough, they may be a huge obstacle to your success.

It's an essential skill to possess since the ramifications of not being able to recognize and effectively manage business deceit can be disastrous. First, it's critical to look at coercive behaviors and develop multiple strategies for handling entities' influence in the workplace.

Persuasion versus Tampering

The majority of people are misinformed, manipulative, and persuasive. Fair coworkers also experience unneeded stress as a result of this misconception.

Generally, just because someone is trying to persuade you to do something doesn't always indicate they're lying to you. Identifying which one it is and acting appropriately are both required.

By its very nature, coercion uses devious, cunning, or even violent methods to try and change the behavior of others. It is different from compulsion since it is evil, coercive, and exploitative.

Conversely, persuasion is trying to influence others to agree with your point of view. It must benefit both parties since it's direct and stems from a sincere concern.

To do this, take a step back and consider the situation from a third-person perspective. Eliminating some preconceived notions and emotions from the situation will assist you in determining whether doing the action will benefit everyone involved or hurt you.

Operate in the gray area.

It might be difficult for some people, especially young ones, to tell if a coworker is trying to intimidate or persuade. Regretfully, manipulators are less likely to be successful—and consequently harmful—the more effective they are.

The majority of citizens have good intentions. However, implicitly trusting a coworker you don't know well in a gray workplace could lead to unfavorable consequences. However, coming across as unduly worried might alienate many people and make your tenure at the company unpleasant, awkward, and unproductive.

Dark Persuasion Strategies To Watch Out For

You should understand why dark persuasion damages the victim after learning about the many forms of persuasion and what they all mean. It might be simpler to comprehend when a manipulator is using you if you know the various strategies they might employ.

So how precisely might a dark persuader use this concept to fulfill their desires? A dark manipulator can employ a variety of strategies, but some of the most popular ones are as follows:

The Protracted Swindle

We will examine the Long Con as our first technique. This approach is a little slow and drawn out, but it can be quite successful because it takes so long and is difficult to identify or even pinpoint the exact moment when anything went wrong. Several factors contribute to an individual's capacity to withstand persuasion, including the perception of pressure exerted by the other person, which may force them to retreat. They will also avoid the individual attempting to convince them if they sense a lack of connection or trust. The Long Con is incredibly successful because they can get beyond these major obstacles and deliver the persuader exactly what they want.

The Long Con gives the evildoer the luxury of winning the victim's trust. They will need to get to know the victim to gain their trust and approval. The persuader will achieve this with artificial rapport building, which often seems excessive, and other approaches that will aid in raising the comfort levels between the persuader and their target.

The persuader will start their attempts as soon as they determine that the victim is psychologically prepared. They might begin by seeming to be persuasive in a favorable way. The persuader will coerce the victim to decide or take certain activities to help the persuader. The persuasive person will benefit from this in two ways. The victim will get accustomed to being persuaded by that person, and then they will mentally associate the persuasion with a favorable result.

The Long Con takes so long to finish because the persuader wants to avoid drawing too much attention to themselves. An illustration of this is the case of a recently widowed woman who is at risk due to her advanced age and her recent loss. A man initiates a friendship with her following her loss. This man could be a relative or someone she knew from church. It doesn't take long for her guard to come down when he shows up because he is becoming more affectionate and patient with her.

The man then begins to perform the previously indicated, smaller acts of positive persuasion. He can suggest a better approach to lower her monthly expenses or which bank account to utilize. When she heeds the counsel, the victim will be grateful for the man's efforts and his attempts to assist her.

The man then tries to employ some devious persuasion after a while. Maybe he'll try to talk her into giving him a portion of her money to invest. Because positive persuasion worked so well in the past, she agrees. The man will undoubtedly work hard to extract as much from her. The money is lost because he simply had poor luck with the investment, but if the manipulator is good enough, she can think he truly wants to help her. This is the limit of dark persuasion.

Gradualism

When we read or hear about acts of dark persuasion, they usually sound implausible and unreal. We overlook that this dark persuasion won't ever be a significant or unexpected request that appears out of the blue. Dark persuasion works better as a staircase; the victim will never be asked to take a major, dramatic step on their first meeting with the dark persuader; instead, the victim will be guided one step at a time.

When the manipulator has the target merely travel one step at a time, the procedure feels less of a huge problem. The victim will likely not be allowed to leave or climb back up again once they have descended, much before they even realize it.

Let's look at an illustration of how this procedure will work in the actual world. Assume that a criminal intended for someone else to carry out their crimes. This is exactly what cult leaders, gang leaders, and even Charles Manson did.

This criminal would never consider asking their victim to murder to start the procedure. Nobody in their right mind would voluntarily go out and kill someone they hardly knew. Thus, this would raise red flags. Rather, the offender would first have the victim do a little offense, such as a petty misdemeanor, or they would just conceal a weapon for them. Something that, in contrast, isn't all that significant for the victim.

The more serious the acts the manipulator can convince their victim to commit, the more time they will spend doing so. Additionally, because they committed the lesser offenses, the persuader now has the invisible power to hold the victim accountable for some of those smaller transgressions, much like in a blackmail situation. The victim will feel like they are too deep before they realize it. After that, they'll be coerced into committing some of the most horrifying crimes. By now, individuals will frequently act this way because they believe they have no other option.

Chapter 5: Control of Thought

The Background of Mind Control and Its Current Consequences

When considering the history of mind control, one may recall the employment of brainwashing methods in prison camps and injurious cults, which have the ability to permanently damage or even kill members of their adherents.

You may also recall headlines about mass suicide, persistent psychological impairment, post-traumatic stress disorder, or Stockholm syndrome. Mind control is still very much a part of daily life, even though we might not always be conscious of it or know when it's happening. The consequences of mind control are not always evident, and they frequently have an unconscious impact on our choices, emotions, and ideas. Mind control has historically been used to create fear and obedience in large groups. It can also exert strong control over an individual or within smaller groups. When this happens, the power dynamic becomes drastically unbalanced in favor of the manipulator(s). Certain governments may maintain control over their population in nations or areas with little freedom or liberty by threatening to arrest, penalize, or otherwise deny them basic rights. Clean water and food frequently fear being punished for speaking up or disobeying because they fear losing what little they have left for their family and communities.

As it has always been, mind control is widely used today. It happens worldwide between smaller groups and people and within governments and institutions.

Though we frequently disregard the warnings, it's more evident and prevalent than ever in many ways. Commercial influence and the capacity to persuade consumers to purchase unnecessary goods are potent tools, particularly when those consumers are prepared to incur debt or forego hard-earned money in favor of less significant purchases. Certain media outlets may broadcast or print particular headlines and occurrences more frequently than others to induce a sense of urgency or panic over home invasion or public safety. They might employ strong language to arouse feelings of shock or terror, making individuals live more watchfully and cautiously and not stray from the "norm."

What Indicates Mental Control?
Like manipulation, mind control seeks an advantage by persuading and influencing an individual or group of individuals' thoughts, actions, and behaviors. People who are readily persuaded and manipulated are more likely to practice or engage in activities they would not ordinarily perceive

viable. The methods employed, the target or targets, and the surrounding circumstances can all affect the outcome or success of mind control. These elements, among others, have a significant impact on the effectiveness and potency of mind control and offer guidance on identifying these warning signals before they worsen:

Separation

Isolation can simply mean being cut off from friends and family, even though this may appear like a severe case of solitary confinement.

An abusive spouse or partner may frequently employ this strategy to prevent their partner from receiving consolation and assistance from friends and relatives. Psychological isolation occurs when a manipulator gradually makes you believe that a family member or family members are attempting to control you. They are the ones in charge. Suppose they convince you over time that your family is dishonest or manipulative. In that case, they might also go after friends, acquaintances, or coworkers, telling you there's something wrong with them or that your friends aren't sincere, jealous, or deserving of your friendship in the first place. Friendships and family eventually take a backseat, and you become more emotionally reliant on the individual using these mind control methods. When you eventually come to understand the risks of being left alone with someone who does not have your best interests at heart, isolation can effectively prevent you from getting help.

Recognizing the subtle but early warning signs of someone or an organization trying to distance you from others is critical to preventing a long-term catastrophe. Any kind of negativity or discrediting of close friends and family members must be taken seriously as a potential indicator of control. This method usually occurs early in a relationship, where the manipulator realizes a strong tie between you and others.

They will stop at nothing to destroy these ties to maintain your subservience to their will since they regard this as challenging their authority over you. A group or organization is trying to take over your life if it seems welcoming and inclusive but still challenges the nature of your friendships and personal ties.

Section 5. Neuro-Linguistic Programming: What Is It?

As the name implies, neuro-linguistic programming, or NLP, consists of three main parts:

neurology. which means nerve, and the suffix "logy," which is derived from the Greek word "logia," which means "study of." Thus, neurology can be defined as the study of nerves. However, according to science, neurology is defined as a branch of medicine that focuses primarily on identifying and managing any conditions directly or indirectly related to the central nervous system.

Words. The term "language" refers to the human communication system that makes sense of abstract and complicated ideas by using any, all, or some of the various modes of expression, such as speaking, writing, or gesturing, to convey inner thoughts or emotions. Language makes the ability to communicate, satiate wants and desires, and create and preserve relationships, cultures, and traditions possible.

Programming. The act of establishing presetbehavioral patterns is referred to as programming. Indeed, programming is the magical link that unites linguistic and neuronal systems. Blending with Neuro-Linguistic gives it a much larger dimension that surpasses any impurities in the mind. It merely makes a map showing the way to the mind's release, releasing it from captivity.

These fundamental definitions of the key terminology prepare us to analyze the main ideas of NLP. Studying and comprehending how individuals organize their thoughts, feelings, communications, and actions to achieve their goals is at the heart of NLP, an art and science.

Simply put, NLP facilitates the analysis of the connections among our mental processes (neuro), language, behavioral and emotional patterns (programs), and behaviors.

The Core Idea of NLP

The core idea of NLP is that people's distinct mental maps of their surroundings result from how they interpret and filter the data gathered by their five senses. In this sense, the term "neuro" refers to the mental map created by a person's particular mental filtering system for processing information detected by their five senses. The senses that make up a person's neurological filtering process include tastes, scents, sounds, internal images, and awareness. This mental map is called "First Access" in NLP jargon.

Linguistics, like neurology, has a special meaning in NLP and is essentially the process of giving personal interpretation to data collected from the environment. A higher level of conscious awareness is the outcome of this linguistic process, which fills the linguistic map by giving a language to sounds, tastes, scents, sensations, and interior images. The second language map in the NLP is this one.

Making mental maps is central to NLP. Yes, every journey you take is about walking on the carpet your mind map creates in front of you. Without a mental blueprint, you can never take a voluntary step. You may be unconsciously acting this way, but it's true nonetheless.

Was Neuro-Linguistic Education Rumored?

There is no scientific proof that neurolinguistic programming is safe and effective. Nevertheless, there are a lot of people that support counseling. The absence of convincing data to back up the research plagues the entire field. However, some contend that the fundamental principles sufficiently support the NLP.

Using a quotation from the Research Digest post, "It is accurate that several psychologists are qualified in neuro-linguistic programming (NLP) and support its use, but it is a significant mistake to think that NLP is based on scientific studies in either psychology or neuroscience. In reality, the method–generally advertised as a way to achieve greater personal achievement–was created by two self-help gurus in the 1970s, who formulated their own therapeutic beliefs by witnessing psychotherapists interact with their clients. NLP is full of false statements that sound scientific-ish, such as that we each have a preferred "representational method" to think about the world and that the easiest way to influence someone is to imitate. The NLP programs found that the overwhelming majority were puffed. In many cases, this may be innocuous, but in 2013, a foundation was called upon to offer NLP-based treatment to traumatized war veterans.

2. The arsonist is there

The arsonist is a person who has an obsession with starting fires; these individuals frequently have a history of abuse, both physical and sexual. It is uncommon for serial arsonists to be lonesome, to have few friends, and to be completely consumed by the act of starting fires. They also tend to be highly ritualistic and to stick to a set of procedures when starting fires.

After their target is set, some arsonists experience sexual arousal and masturbation while watching. Despite their obsessive and ritualistic behavior, the prolific arsonist is proud of his acts. Arsonists are worried about starting a fire. They also fantasize and concentrate on how to design their fire-setting scenes.

3. A fascination with corpses

Necrophilia, necrology, and thanatophobia all refer to the same type of disordered person: men, and there are men like these, who are attracted to bodies sexually. Paraphilia is a psychological term used to describe a person's sexual arousal and affection for things, situations, or people that are not part of normal stimulation and may cause them distress or grave issues. Therefore, paraphilia of the Necrophile is the sexual excitement of a deceased person.

Perceived power is the primary need for Necrophiles, and experts who have compiled profiles of these men show how difficult it is for them to experience the capacity to be intimate with others. In tests, Necrophiles demonstrated a strong sense of control when they were with a corpse. A sense of connection is less important to these men than the need for perceived power.

4. A prolific murderer

A true human killer, or serial killer, is someone who kills three or more victims in 30 days or less. Most serial killers interviewed indicated that they had a cooling-off period between each murder, which is a cognitive refractory phase in which they are temporarily satisfied with their need to inflict pain on other people.

Researchers in the field of criminal psychology have concluded that the motivation behind murder is the creation of an encounter of personal pleasure that can only be experienced through violence. Following a murder, some people experience a combination of egotistical strength and empowerment. Practice makes them feel so good that they will experience freedom and pleasure again.

The FBI is often interested in sexual assault, abuse, embarrassment, and coercion in the course of their murders. Federal Bureau of Investigation experts outlined motivations besides anger, rage, attention-seeking, thrill-seeking, and monetary gain. Serial killers frequently have similar patterns in their choice of victims, how they destroy their targets and strategies for disposing of the body. Criminal analysts specializing in behavioral analysis of multiple serial killers have a background of significant emotional, criminal, and psychological trauma.

In addition to having mild to severe counselors, these four examples of criminals and criminal classes performing coercive and/or violent odd crimes have deep psychological disorders and skewed worldviews in common. Can metastasize their entire being and challenge reason. What about these human predators? How do they act and socialize in their daily lives? Such short portraits speak volumes of the bleak nature of the human experience.

The serial arsonist may not be a violent person or enjoy acting as a sexual predator, unlike the serial killer. However, he still gets pleasure and happiness from starting his fire. He also feels a sense of accomplishment from the destruction he has caused. His fire-setting incidents are very dangerous, as long as they don't threaten others, but he doesn't do it to cause damage or bodily harm.

Securing

As previously discussed, anchoring bears similarities to Pavlov's dog studies. It is also worthwhile to condition ourselves since failing can cause us to lose our identity, become accustomed to our routines, and fail to recognize that someone controls, for example, the structure of our workdays.

Reactions to experiences and events are combined in anchoring. A crucial factor in the anchoring case is the neurological system. Become a conscious person and steer your anchors. Have a genuine impact on your feelings and response to a particular event. When dealing with an anchor, it's critical to make the situation more severe. Now, learn to let go of the states that support you and transform your objectives into an alluring vision.

We can define anchors as symbols that cause us to experience particular emotions. To positively impact our nervous system and brain, we do not necessarily need to understand every detail of how it works. Everybody has felt both good and bad at some point in their lives. Although we wish to move past these unpleasant feelings immediately, they are associated with a specific pattern. For instance, even though we dislike feeling timid or uneasy, when we recall such an event, we unintentionally enter that mood and respond accordingly in future similar circumstances. For this reason, it is worthwhile to employ anchors to break this pattern and to deliberately be calm, stress-free, and self-assured in tense situations.

Our behavior and responses to the outside world shape how others see us. Sometimes, all it takes is a gesture or technique to effortlessly recall bits and pieces of the past, an instance that sets off the ideal states in us—exactly the ones we require in a certain circumstance. When it comes to anchoring, it is crucial to design a new one that is permanent rather than just temporary, requiring a specific system to function. When designing a new anchor, it's crucial to consider the strength of your feelings as you install it, its clarity, how it breaks the pattern, what makes it unique, and how much of an oddity it has to set it apart from other events you can draw from memory or that have happened in the past. The moment the anchor is put on is also crucial because it intensifies the impressions that will help people remember it better.

How successful are methods of mind control?

The efficiency of mind control is dependent on a few elements. For example, the degree of influence depends on the method employed. Additional elements consist of;

- How frequently does the victim encounter the methods?
- How long someone is exposed to the procedures, • Whether hypnosis or hypnotic mind control is employed,

The number of techniques employed at any given time, the degree of direct interaction between the victim and the perpetrator, the manipulator's ability, and the existence of additional physical tactics used to persuade and manipulate, such as sexual abuse

- Whether the person is getting support from other people who can perceive the intents of the manipulator.

Here are a few instances to show how successful mind control can be. In comparison to someone who spends only two hours a week with a manipulator, the impact of mind control will be greater if a person has a manipulative spouse, lives in the same home, spends a lot of time together, shares a lot of information, and has little social interaction. A victim who spends more time with their victimizer will experience more effects than a victim who spends very little time with them.

All the focus is on one individual for those who are part of one-on-one manipulation cults, especially if there is an intimate relationship involved, like a husband and wife. The methods employed can have very disastrous effects. These days, the phrase "complex trauma" is used to characterize the experiences of children and young adults raised by psychopathic and narcissistic parents.

Given the current situation of the globe, it is understandable why more individuals are searching for safety and acceptance in the middle of chaos. Most people find isolation and exclusion unsettling, which makes them vulnerable to mind control and manipulation. The victim will continue to stray into the fake world as long as the manipulator appears to be providing an answer to a specific issue.

Decision-making and mental control

Making decisions is crucial in daily life. No matter how big or small your decision, it will ultimately define your success. Remember that the manipulator dictates what you do while giving the impression that you are in control. Therefore, it's critical to understand how to respond to them.

Some people cringe at choosing, while others sigh in excruciating pain. Other people will do whatever to dodge decision-making. Others know what they are doing is right, but they are terrified of taking the fallout and failing for it. Put simply, most people want to place the blame elsewhere so that, should they fail, they can blame peer pressure for their actions.

A person needs to be able to make decisions in one or two ways at work. This won't always ensure success, but it will at least make things easier and prevent manipulation. However, the question of whether to make decisions rationally or intuitively emerges. That will depend on the circumstances. You may occasionally need to make decisions quickly, while others will call for more thought and consideration. Therefore, before making a decision, you must comprehend the circumstances.

You will also need to continuously think about methods to sharpen your decision-making abilities to lower your stress levels and save money, time, and effort. The more adept you are at making decisions, the more you will be able to resist persuasion. You must comprehend mental manipulation and control to make better decisions. Is it possible that someone is making decisions for you while giving you the impression that you are in control? Someone may be making choices for you while maintaining your sense of independence. That's what you should stay away from.

Mind control and manipulation

In all honesty, life is full of good and negative decisions. There are choices we never make. Most circumstances when decision-making abilities are required present a range of options. And conflict stems from these choices. We frequently find ourselves divided between options, trying to select the best. However, Making the choice does not always mean that the conflict will be resolved, particularly if our expectations are unmet. Making decisions requires letting go of some potentially wise decisions in favor of others. Additionally, there is pressure to resolve the issue and make the best decision. While you can take steps to improve the process, it is not always simple.

Knowing what you stand for and using it as a guide will help you take charge of your life and success and stay free from manipulation. Never let any piece of information that someone gives you influence you. Personal decision-making is crucial, particularly in the face of error. In a technical sense, making wise decisions is the key to success. Experience is necessary for making wise decisions, and experience is gained from making poor choices and failing at things. Therefore, you shouldn't be afraid to make mistakes because doing so will only sharpen your intuition.

Advice on how to make excellent decisions without coercion

The most popular guidelines for decision-making are listed here, and you should consider them before choosing. When the time comes, you'll find it easier to decide if you take note of the concepts and understand these recommendations. While some of the advice presented here may go against popular belief, some of the best decision-makers successfully apply it. Making better decisions and living a better life are achieved by applying these principles for decision-making.

First tip: You are the best.

You will be impacted by every choice, either directly or indirectly. You must prioritize yourself since you are highly important. It is crucial that the choices you make lead to an improvement in your life. Even if it may sound self-serving, it is preferable to take care of yourself than to live your entire life in the shadow of other people. As the saying goes, you can only give what you have, and it does no one good if your life is filled with regrettable choices. Before you share, take some time to accomplish the things you want to do for yourself.

Keep in mind that prioritizing oneself does not entail disregarding others. It indicates that you have taken sufficient care of yourself to be useful to others. Of course, you can go above and beyond once in a while to help others, but only after asking if they would reciprocate. Take your time to work things out if your partner can't go above and beyond to support you. The most significant thing in your life is you, and the likelihood of being duped increases when you are not well.

The Real Story of Hypnosis

One of the most misinterpreted or contentious psychiatric interventions is hypnosis. People's preconceptions of stage hypnosis are mostly responsible for the myths and misconceptions surrounding hypnotherapy. In actuality, stage hypnosis is nothing more than a theatrical production, and it differs from genuine therapeutic hypnosis in the same way that many Hollywood productions differ from actual life.

However, the truth remains that hypnosis is a legitimate psychological occurrence with practical uses in medical settings. Hypnosis, to put it simply, is a highly concentrated state of attention or concentration that is frequently accompanied by relaxation and increased suggestibility. Those who are hypnotized or in a hypnotic state appear to be far more receptive to constructive advice than they often are.

"Post-hypnotic suggestions" are positive suggestions offered to a person while they are hypnotized; this is because they have to take effect after the person exits the trance or is no longer hypnotized.

Suggestions to hypnotized individuals have a significant role in the process's mechanics. Under hypnosis, ideas seem to find their way into the mind—possibly through the back door of consciousness—even though many people do not accept or react to direct suggestions. They frequently begin as significant behavioral and psychological shifts that sprout or take hold.

Those who are hypnotized, in contrast to the common misconception, have total control over themselves and will never do anything that they would normally find extremely undesirable.

Furthermore, not everyone is enchanted; it is a fact. The quality known as "hypnotizability," which, like other qualities, varies widely between individuals, appears to be possessed by some people. A person needs to be at least moderately hypnotized and willingly go through this process to be successfully hypnotized.

Hypnotherapy is ineffective for anyone, not even deeply hypnotized individuals, and one hypnosis session seldom yields long-lasting effects. A person frequently has to go through a series of hypnotic exercises to support any helpful advice that is offered.

Hypnosis is most frequently used in professional settings to help patients break undesirable habits, relieve sleeplessness, recall lost memories, and reduce discomfort.

Testing the advantages of self-hypnosis is simple. Simply choose a quiet place to sit or lie down and get comfortable. After that, close your eyes and inhale and exhale deeply many times. Many people experience a mild trance and a relaxed, comfortable feeling. Talk positively to yourself in this mood (e.g., "I will easily miss dessert") and conjure up nice memories (e.g., an image of victory). Even a five-minute session can be helpful for certain folks.

How Do You Use Hypnosis?

German physician Franz Mesmer, who gained notoriety in the 1700s for "fascinating his patients," was banished from city to city for lying. The locals think his method of putting the person in a blissful condition through persuasion is a ruse.

But as of right now, Messmer has been validated: Numerous studies have demonstrated that hypnotism is real, and hypnotists are now accepted members of the psychology community.

As to the Stanford Hypnosis Susceptibility Scale, most individuals exhibit a "hypnotic effect" to some extent. People are ranked from 0 to 12 on a Stanford University psychologists' scale according to how much they follow the hypnotist's advice.

On the Stanford University Scale, 5% of participants did not respond to hypnotic suggestions, earning them a score of 0. A smaller sample of respondents achieved the maximum score of 12 by answering all of these questions. One member of the group is so deeply hypnotized that he refuses to record the ammonia smell under his nose even after the hypnotist tells him to switch off sensations. Inhale.

Most people fall between 5 and 7 on the Stanford scale. People have constant hypnotic sensitivity throughout their adult lives, much like their IQ. This, along with the observation that evaluations for identical twins frequently match, suggests that hypnosis is a natural and genetic feature of the human mind.

Putting Hypnosis and Staging It

These days, there are two primary uses for this quality: "phase hypnosis," when a hypnotist causes volunteers to look in a stupor before asking them to carry out absurd activities (such as clucking like a chicken) to draw in the audience, and honored the use of hypnosis. Harvard Medical School hypnotist Deirdre Barrett has authored multiple articles about hypnosis techniques. She begins with thoughtful recommendations that can instantly calm you down, including "Make your breathing slow and deep; let all the tension radiate from your body..."

Barrett stated in "Psychology Today": "The hypnosis tr itself is not therapeutic, but the specific suggestions and images provided to clients can profoundly change their behavior."

Barrett employs hypnotherapy to assist her patients in quitting smoking and losing weight, to mention just two instances. This technique has even been employed by Mount Sinai School of

Medicine, oncologists to shorten the recovery period for surgically repaired breast cancer patients.

Idea of Deceptive Emotional Control

Manipulators concentrate on this area of influence because they know that a person's emotions are fundamental to every other aspect of their personality. It is equivalent to severing someone's jugular vein to manipulate their emotions. A person can manage their emotions if they possess emotional control. The word "coercion" is the last piece of this puzzle. There is a common misperception that power and manipulation are interchangeable concepts. It isn't like that. The term "manipulation" describes devious tactics and covert influencing processes apart from the subject's regulated consciousness. The goal of persuading someone else, as opposed to the intention of controlling them, is another important distinction. An influential person has the perspective of "I want to support you and make choices that are beneficial for you." The mindset of a manipulator is, "I want to subtly manipulate you to favor me." As a result, determining the motivation behind any behavior only requires assessing if it suggests covert emotional manipulation. We've now covered the definition of covert emotional coercion and whether it differs from other forms of control. I will now examine the most common scenarios in which covert emotional manipulation may occur, as well as the main categories of manipulative personalities that recur frequently.

Manipulators in Various Contexts

Indirect exploitation of emotions can happen in four basic contexts: personal, romantic, familial, and professional. Romantic Covert Emotional Manipulation is the most prevalent and potentially lethal scenario. On the other hand, less obvious CEM forms are present practically everywhere. No matter your situation, you'll be able to protect against it once you understand the concept and its useful applications. Just as there are common situations in which emotional manipulation might be done covertly, there are also common types of individuals who generate the concepts that are the basis of CEM. To grasp the CEM theory completely, one must relate it to authentic, unique representations of its ideas. One commonly cited example of a CEM principle in action is a controlling life partner.

When a person is in a marriage and feels like their husband is controlling them, it's natural for them to feel disgusted by the situation and want to escape. As a result, many regulatory partners use the most covert methods to carry out their actions. Their spouse or girlfriend frequently becomes the victim of severe sexual abuse without them even realizing it. As a result, the manipulator has the authority they desire without worrying about being discovered or negatively impacting the other person. Furthermore, a so-called "buddy" could employ CEM to manipulate the other person into giving them what they desire from their relationship. In this particular category, one of the most common types of manipulators is someone who purposefully arouses feelings of guilt, empathy, and accountability in others. When someone is manipulated this way, they won't be aware of it. They refuse to explain their feelings and behaviors toward their "friend," the manipulator. The Professional Field is another common playground for emotional tricksters that operate covertly. Numerous people have experiences working for a boss or some prominent figure that appeared to induce strange feelings about sorrow, fear, or duty. Individuals who have experienced this kind of abuse have never been able to pinpoint the cause or genesis of those feelings. Family situations are among the most concerning in the field of CEM.

An extremely dangerous manipulator in terms of influence is adept at finding a victim inside their own family. CEM is a useful strategy, especially when there is no clear relationship between the manipulator and the target. Adding the genuine bond, the blood link, will significantly increase the degree of power and leverage. Why are family issues a good fit for the application of CEM? To put it plainly, people today feel a moral need to help those not members of their own family to "go the extra mile" and see to it that their needs are satisfied. The effect is a relatively soft target, and the underlying emotional manipulation activities add to the current tendency toward control. How exactly do covert mind controllers maintain this amount of victim power instillation? They employ several tricky tactics that are difficult to identify but much harder to avoid.

Techniques

You are already familiar with the idea of subliminal emotional manipulation and the kinds of situations in which it will occur. This provides a good overall overview of the subject. Still, it also has to consider some of the various methods that manipulators employ to increase their influence. The whole purpose of this type of emotional abuse is to make it as difficult to detect as possible. This chapter intends to reveal this hidden world to everyone.

Love Bombing: Relational manipulators frequently employ this strategy when starting a relationship with a target. It includes the seemingly paradoxical act of really, unexpectedly, and aggressively expressing positive thoughts toward a victim. Why do people act so intensely positively right away if they aim to harm other people? Since it serves a function! The theory behind love bombing is that it gives the victim's manipulator an overpowering sense of confidence, closeness, and loyalty. The manipulator's evaluation of the circumstance determines the extent of the love bombing as well as the targets of the technique. A manipulator will more thoroughly and freely show affection to a target who is depressed, alone, and in need of support because they believe that the target will respond to it.

Similarly, a target with greater roots would require a milder and more nuanced positivity attack. One can gain two key lessons about CEM from the description of the practice of love bombing. Firstly, it eloquently illustrates CEM's concealed presence.

Reinforcement: In the textbook, a typical CEM scenario consists of love bombing, upbeat Strengthening, and sporadic positive attention. This is the clarification of the reasoning behind this order. Early in a relationship, a love bombing is a lucid, naive, and exaggerated display of optimism from a manipulator to a victim. It is intended to undermine a victim's defenses, increase their reliance on the manipulator, and provide the framework for a close relationship or other forms of supportive collaboration. After love-bombing, the next move is always constructive affirmation. This is a reversal of behavior in which the manipulator stops exhibiting constant, unwavering enthusiasm toward their target.

Refusing to acknowledge Reality: Feeling as though one is losing one's mind is among the most agonizing experiences one can go through. This is disturbing enough if the cause is something clear, like a mental illness or a transient side effect of pressure. Still, it becomes even more so if an emotional manipulator subtly creates the feeling of insanity. Reality denial is a term used to describe various CEM techniques that have the similar objective of weakening a person's morality to forward the manipulator's goals. We will now delve deeper into the process of reality denial and its consequences. One of the main ideas supporting the rejection of truth is gradualism. Since it is hard to achieve without being detected, manipulators are unlikely to aim for the whole destruction of a target's well-being in the first place. Rather, the skilled manipulators follow the process "slowly but steadily." This entails a person's health gradually deteriorating until their faith in their abilities is based on the thinnest of grounds.

www.ingramcontent.com/pod-product-compliance
Lightning Source LLC
Chambersburg PA
CBHW052143110526
44591CB00012B/1837